Fellow-citizens, we cannot escape history. We of this Congress and this administration will be remembered in spite of ourselves. No personal significance, or insignificance, can spare one or another of us. The fiery trial through which we pass will light us down, in honor or dishonor, to the latest generation.

A. Lincoln
Second Annual Message
December 1, 1862

MISTER LINCOLN

A drama in two acts

By Herbert Mitgang

SOUTHERN ILLINOIS UNIVERSITY PRESS
Carbondale and Edwardsville

For my clan, Esther, Lee and Gina, and Laura;
and for my sisters, Harriet and Phyllis.

Library of Congress Cataloging in Publication Data

Mitgang, Herbert.
  Mister Lincoln.

  Contents: Act I, The advocate—Act II, The liberator.
    1. Lincoln, Abraham, 1809–1865—Drama. I. Title.
PS3563.183M5   812'.54   81–8895
ISBN 0–8093–1034–1   AACR2

Introduction

By Herbert Mitgang

In writing *Mister Lincoln* for the theatre, I decided from the start that a one-man play would be ideal for my subject and concept. I was aware that this form had been evolving in recent years; that what had to be avoided was a feeling by the audience that it was watching a play with a lectern at dead center for high-minded speeches. I had seen most of the current one-man plays and found that those I admired were most dramatized, most theatrical.

Why, I wondered, did some personages—political or literary—work better than others in a monodrama? I felt that it had to do with language rather than actions; that the theatre is still a self-contained area of eloquence where words count. The words have to come first; without them the finest actor must falter.

Lincoln, whose life I had studied for many years, happened to have been the best writer who ever occupied the White House. And I believe that we can place him in the front rank of American writers outside the White House, too. Who else could say: "They are blowing out the moral lights around us" or call upon

Americans "to bind up the nation's wounds"? Measured against modern presidents, it is important to realize that his words were hand-fashioned without a single ghost writer or pollster to guide his pen or thought.

It struck me that the one-man form could serve as a concentrate for Lincoln's language without distillation or distraction. It would mean that the dialogue of everyday life, the hesitations and doubts, could also advance the character portrait in a human way. I still wanted to achieve the Aristotelian unities of action, time and place; I aimed to do so by making thematic connections between life-incidents. As in a novel, one can plant certain ideas in early chapters—the first act—that can be called to mind and pay off at the end—in the second act.

And so, as the play took shape in my mind, I was forced to think harder on Lincoln and the centrality of his life than I had ever done before as a Lincoln biographer or film documentarian. The central theme that emerged was his own evolving stand on slavery that led to the Emancipation Proclamation. "If I ever get a chance to hit the Institution," he says in Act I, "I'm going to hit it hard." With his Proclamation in Act II as a high moment, he does. Although it is difficult for some people to realize it today, slavery, not civil rights, was the issue in the Civil War era. There were men, women and children—families—in bondage, bought and sold as chattels. This straightforward, horrible fact helped to structure the forward motion that *Mister Lincoln* would take in its serious elements.

There were other things I wished to say about Lincoln's mind and main positions. I particularly felt great admiration for his stand against the Mexican War—he was a "dove" and blamed the invasion on the Americans, not the Mexicans—which was unpopular with his Illinois constituents and friends. Because he was against that war and against militarism—"that attractive rainbow, rising in showers of blood"—he was denied a chance to run for Congress a second time. That took guts, and foresight, for a man too often branded a mere politician. For our own age of military domination of the national budget and therefore of our lives, I wanted to underscore Lincoln's antimilitarism dramatically.

Although the one-man form appeared ideal to get across the Lincoln character and literature, I found myself at war with my own knowledge. Biography is not drama; drama is not necessarily biography. To Lincoln scholars, daily events and specific incidents are of vital importance. Perhaps that is why the great Lincoln biographers—James Randall, Benjamin Thomas, Allan Nevins, Carl Sandburg—never attempted to write a play about him. Yet a man's stage life differs from his biographical life. Time is shortened and heightened in the theatre; the clock and the clockworks run differently.

To avoid that old lecture-platform look, I had to leave out significant parts of the Lincoln-Douglas debates. I had to omit one of my favorite events, Lincoln's Cooper Union speech in New York, that helped to get him the nomination for president. Lucky for the country, unlucky for me, the great Second Inaugural Address came too soon after the great Gettysburg Address. Something had to give or the stage would turn into a textbook; it was I who gave through selection.

That is why I made sure to include an Author's Note in the theatrical playbill that reads: "This is a dramatization of Lincoln's life and mind. Artistic license is necessarily taken in narrative reconstruction, but all the events and ideas in the play are rooted in historical records and personal discoveries. Certain dialogue is newly created; it is based on informed *interpretation* of Lincoln's character and of the times in which he lived. Some of the set pieces and language of the literary Lincoln are not necessarily in chronological sequence, but reflect his spoken or written views faithfully."

I did not want to be drummed out of the vast Lincoln Union of Scholars.

The structure of the one-man form of necessity forced me to create language of my own for Lincoln to speak in the first person. No one was present when he spoke intimately to his wife. No one recorded conversations with his physician. Even some of the main incidents of his presidency, such as his cabinet meetings and visit to the captured capital of the Confederacy, depended on the recollections of others, sometimes long after the events. Lincoln himself was no diarist.

How much of the language is Lincoln's and how much is mine? I have not attempted to measure the play, line by line, since I was more concerned with revealing personality and incident by weaving words and ideas seamlessly. Perhaps the best answer to the question can be found in Brooks Atkinson's defense of Robert Sherwood's *Abe Lincoln in Illinois* in 1939:

> To say that some of the best lines are Lincoln's and not Sherwood's seems to me a microscopic objection. Out of all the mass of Lincolniana, Mr. Sherwood has discovered exalted thoughts that flow naturally into his portrait of one of the world's great men and that illuminate and clarify men's minds at this troubled moment in history. It is very much to Mr. Sherwood's credit that he has assimilated the character of Lincoln so thoroughly and had the wisdom to distinguish the immortal parts of it from the transitory. What was Mr. Sherwood to do—rewrite Lincoln? No, this objection puts playwrighting on a purely sportsmanship basis with the

implication that it is not cricket to use lines not invented by the author for the occasion.

I could not offend the spirit and tone of Lincoln's language even though it did not disturb me one whit that I knew—and the audience and reader would know—that Lincoln never said certain words in the play. For example, after General Grant allows General Lee's defeated officers and soldiers to take home their horses and mules for spring plowing, as a means of bringing about reconciliation, Lincoln says: "It was a time to plant seeds, not men, in the American soil." Lincoln never said it; but that was the idea. I wished to punctuate the ending of the Civil War and hint at what Reconstruction might have been like had Lincoln lived.

There is a cabinet meeting in the play that is used not as exposition but as a revelation about Lincoln's firmness. Did such a cabinet meeting actually take place as I have written it? I doubt it, though participants have recalled certain lively cabinet meetings. However, a similar cabinet vote, where Lincoln was in a minority of one, presumably involved a conscription bill. Conscription bills were highly complex and contradictory during the Civil War; they included the use of substitutes and financial inducements for enlistment. Such an issue would have required too much explaining—the biographer's role. I decided to change the subject of the meeting to habeas corpus. I wanted to show that Lincoln, a lawyer who had invoked the doctrine himself in criminal defense cases, suspended habeas corpus while president—a contradiction in his libertarian views. It allowed me to use a double metaphor of revealing Lincoln's main goal—saving the Union under the Constitution even if it meant violating one of its precepts during a rebellion—and disclosing his toughness as president and commander-in-chief. I did not want to portray him as a wooly-headed, soft figure or as a larger-than-life president in granite but as a human being.

In "The Intent of the Artist," Thornton Wilder wrote that despite directors, actors or other collaborators in the theatre, fundamentally it is the playwright's vision that must prevail:

> The gathered audience sits in a darkened room, one end of which is lighted. The nature of the transaction at which it is gazing is a succession of events illustrating a general idea—the stirring of the idea; the gradual feeding out of information; the shock and counter-shock of circumstances; the flow of action; the interruption of act; the moment of allusion to earlier events; the preparation of surprise, dread, or delight—all that is the author's and his alone.

The one-man form has broken away from the lectern of Charles Dickens and Mark Twain, or the simple readings and elocution lessons, and grown into a play. Although I like the word monodrama, it does not describe *Mister Lincoln* or other challenging dramatizations in this form. For what some of us have tried to do is create many characters through concentrated language and performance by a skilled actor who can command a stage alone. The aim for the audience is to see the unseen, to let its imagination soar beyond time in that lighted place at the end of the theatre.

MISTER LINCOLN

Mister Lincoln by Herbert Mitgang had its world premiere at the Citadel Theatre, Edmonton, Canada, on October 10, 1979, starring British actor Roy Dotrice, and thereafter played at the Hart House Theatre, Toronto, in December 1979. It opened in the United States at Ford's Theatre, Washington, D. C., on January 14, 1980. The play's New York premiere was at the Morosco Theatre on Broadway, February 25, 1980.

In July 1980, *Mister Lincoln* toured in western Australia, playing at His Majesty's Theatre, Perth, and in August 1980, at the Opera Theatre, Adelaide.

On February 9, 1981, *Mister Lincoln,* was presented as the first Hallmark Hall of Fame drama on the Public Broadcasting Service in the United States.

Mister Lincoln opened in a fourth country—Great Britain—on April 22, 1981, at the Fortune Theatre, London.

ACT I | *The Advocate*

The Time, the Scene

At the beginning, it is that fateful moment in the land when, in Whitman's words, "lilacs last in the door-yard bloom'd, and the great star early droop'd in the western sky in the night." Then, suddenly, it is daylight, in the early life of Lincoln and of the Republic, and a respite and recollection, spanning his maturing and presidential years: the fiery trial.

In the first act, he is mainly in Illinois, an advocate; in the second act, he is in Washington, a liberator.

The scene remains the same in both acts. In general, the right side of the stage is for legal and official business; the left side, for relaxing at home, changes of dress, comings and goings; center stage, for public events and speeches; downstage, for direct address to the audience.

The set and the props are best left simple; the authenticity derives from the dialogue. At most, the set can include, at stage right, a table, revolving chair, rolltop desk, railing; stage left, an easy chair, newspaper rack, hallstand with mirror; downstage center, a bench; upstage center, a podium fronted by a bookshelf with well-worn leather-bound volumes of legal and constitutional history.

There are a number of places for moves and moods: Easy chair for feet-up relaxing at home in Springfield or in the White House private quarters; rolltop desk for his law office; table for doctor's office, Oval Office, cabinet meeting; podium for major speeches—campaigns, debates, inaugurals; bench downstage for audience confidences.

Lincoln commands the stage alone in both acts, but there are scores of other characters, private and public, he encounters in the play. They are visible in the audience's imagination.

There is no curtain. The stage darkens. In the background, civil war era tunes are heard. Then a light illuminates the seated figure of Lincoln. Mood music swells, and fades. For a few moments, the time is April 14, 1865.

Lincoln

The calendar called it Good Friday. Washington had never looked more beautiful to Mary and me. The lilacs bursting on their branches outside the White House, the air fragrant with their blossoms, the promise of a new spring—the first spring, for over four years, without the Civil War. And the calendar called it Good Friday.

The battles and the bloodshed of the deadliest, costliest war to civilized humankind, up to that time, were over. Bull Run, Vicksburg, Gettysburg, Atlanta—names on the land, North and South, long remembered as the flaming scenes of war.

I knew then that we could not escape history; that we would be remembered in spite of ourselves. That the fiery trial through which we had passed would light us down, in honor or dishonor, to the latest generation.

The calendar called it Good Friday. And it was a time of renewal, of relaxation. That night I was attending a play with Mary and some friends, seated in the presidential box. Mister Lincoln's, as they called it.

We awaited the next scene. In the shadows behind me, another man waited, his mind a fusebox of hatred, primed to explode. In one hand he carried a single-shot Derringer, in the other a steel dagger. He sighted along the barrel and less than five feet from me, pulled the trigger. The 44-caliber lead ball entered my head. It crossed obliquely into my brain and lodged in my right eye.

The assassin cried out: "Thus be it ever to tyrants!"

And the calendar called it Good Friday.

At that blinding moment, I could see myself very clearly, as a young man, penniless and homeless. . . .

He gets up from chair slowly and steps downstage, walking about

In those days, I was nothing more than a piece of floating driftwood, stranded in the village of New Salem, Illinois. Now some people have tried to make more of me and of my beginnings but it's a great piece of folly to try. It can all be condensed in one single sentence and you'll find it in Gray's *Elegy*: "The short and simple annals of the poor."

From both my parents, I inherited two things: an iron constitution, and a decent poverty. My people, who were Quakers, came over from England before the Declaration of Independence. It was pioneering country then. Grandfather Abraham was killed by Indians while farming. I never did know too much about who my grandfather was—I was always more concerned about what his grandson might become.

In fact, one of my first, though perhaps not my most inspired, pieces of poetry I wrote in my exercise book at the ripe old age of eight:

> "Abraham Lincoln is my name,
> And with my pen I wrote the same;
> I wrote in both haste and speed,
> And left it here for fools to read;
> Abraham Lincoln, his hand and pen,
> He will be good, but God knows when."

I started out life as a migrant farm laborer, working for a day's pay here and there. I remember a farmer, James Taylor, once asked me if I could kill a hog. I said "If you're willing to risk the hog, I'm willing to risk myself."

My father taught me to work, but he never taught me to love it.

He steps on bench

I earned my first pair of trousers splitting rails. "Say, Mrs. Miller! If I split some rails for you, will you give me some yardage of brown jeans? You will? How many for how much? Four-hundred split rails for one yard! Mrs. Miller, with my altitude, I doubt if there are enough rails in Illinois to construct my pantaloons!"

So many people had commented about the length of my legs that I began to wonder, how long should a man's legs be in proportion to the rest of his body? Thinking it over carefully, I delivered myself of a learned opinion: A man's lower limbs, in order to preserve harmony of proportion, should be at least long enough to reach from his body to the ground!

He hangs up jacket at hallstand, then goes to bookshelf

When I came of age, I didn't know too much. Oh, I had a little formal learning in a "blab school"—education by repetition. I was interested in grammar and the English language—the only language, unfortunately, that I ever learned. I could read, write and cipher to the rule of three, but that was about all. Any advance I now have on this store of learning, I picked up under the pressure of necessity.

Back in the village of New Salem, anybody who gave me a book became my best friend. I was a diligent student of Shakespeare: To know the Bard can be a liberal education. And, among other poets, Robert Burns is my inseparable companion—a people's poet.

He takes a small book of Burns' poetry from his coat pocket, but recites from memory

> Give fools their silks, and knaves their wine,
> A man's a man for all that.
> For all that, and all that,
> Their tinsel show, and all that;
> The honest man, tho' e'er sae poor,
> Is king of men for all that.

I find it very hard to scratch anything on this brain of mine but almost impossible to rub it out once it gets there.

Over the years, I collected a number of anecdotes, or "Lincoln stories," as my neighbors call them. Mind you, I didn't make the stories mine just by telling them. I was only a *retail* dealer. But I needed them sometimes to disarm an opponent or as a labor-saving device to save a long-winded argument, and I needed them to get me out of my occasional bouts of melancholy. Oh yes; I have them, too. And I always found a story most effective when I told it against myself.

Now that reminds me of a story. I was over in Decatur, listening to a gentleman-banker lecture on the virtues of the capitalist-banking system. He went on and on, freely giving away words of advice, without charging one penny interest. When he finished, I heckled him and he asked my name. "Oh, so you're Abraham Lincoln," he said. Well, I had to admit I was. "They tell me,

Mister Lincoln, that you're a self-made man." I confessed what there was of me was indeed self-made. "Well, Mister Lincoln, in that case, all I have to say is, it was a damn bad job!"

He picks up Journal from rack near chair

You know he wasn't the first, and by no means the last, to criticize me and my appearance. I remember many years later when I was in the White House that Edward Dicey, a journalist from England, wrote an article about me in the *London Spectator*, in which he said, "Mister Lincoln wore an ill-fitting suit of black, creased and soiled and puckered up at every salient point in the figure."

He folds paper crossing up to hallstand; when audience reacts he turns to them

Oh, so you agree with Mr. Dicey. Well, then let me read you this verse, one of my favorite pieces of poetry. It was composed by a southern minister.

ABRAHAM LINCOLN

His cheek bones were high and his
visage was rough,
Like a mid'ling of bacon, all wrinkled
and tough,
His nose was as long, and as ugly
and big
As the snout of a half-starved
Illinois pig.

Well, you can tell he was a minister; why, that just reeks of the Lord's charity.

He puts on hat and coat and picks up umbrella. He moves to stage left of the bench, which is now an auction block

You know, all men and women have certain turning points in their lives, flashes of wisdom buried deep in their minds. I have often wondered what turned Abraham Lincoln against slavery in his youth. Thinking back on it, I believe it was the slave auctions I witnessed with my own eyes when I was working as a flatboatman, poling a raft of goods down the Mississippi River. Near the riverbank in New Orleans, I saw dealers in human degradation, selling men and women like so many hogs.

On the block was a beautiful girl called Eliza. A Frenchman from New Orleans bid $1,200 for her but his bid was topped by a young Methodist minister. The auctioneer pulled the dress from Eliza's shoulders, exposing her breasts, and said: "Who's gonna lose a chance like this?" The sweating Frenchman bid $1,465, once again the young minister outbid him. The auctioneer lifted Eliza's dress, baring her body from her feet to her waist, slapped her on the thigh, and said: "Who's gonna win this prize?" The Frenchman bid $1,580, the auctioneer raised his gavel, the girl looked at the minister in terror and pleading. He bid $1,585.

He strikes handle of umbrella against bench like auctioneer

The gavel came down, and the girl fell in a faint. The auctioneer said: "Well sir, you got her damn cheap. What are you gonna do with her?" The young minister, whose name was Fairbanks, and who was one of the leaders of the anti-slavery movement in Ohio, said: "Free her!"

I have since learned that Fairbanks has spent seventeen years in the state penitentiary for his antislavery activities. Mind you, he was one of the lucky ones. In the Southern states, leaders of slavery revolts could and had been hanged.

He sits on bench

I saw a "gentleman" who had bought twelve Negroes in different parts of Kentucky, taking them to his farm in the South. Each Negro had an iron clevis around his left wrist, which was fastened by means of a short chain to the main chain, so that every slave was strung up. There they were like so many fish on a line. And in this condition, they were being separated forever from their parents, from their wives, from their children, going into perpetual slavery, where the lash of the master is ruthless and unrelenting.

I learned another lesson during my youth in New Salem—that Abraham Lincoln was not cut out to be a professional soldier.

Well, would you believe I was a military man once? Oh yes sir, I fought, bled and came away unscathed. I didn't break my sword, because I had none to break, but I bent my musket pretty badly.

He twirls his umbrella, imitating manual of arms

I became a military man for the reason that has inspired many an enlistment in the name of patriotism—I had nothing better to do. You see, there was some trouble between the Indians and settlers in Northwest Illinois. I volunteered for thirty days. The

Clary's Grove boys, back in the Village of New Salem, elected me captain—an honor that gave me more satisfaction than any other subsequent success in my life.

They were no easy bunch of boys to drill into obeying orders. And I was an amateur myself. I remember one occasion, I just couldn't think of the order to pass two platoons endwise, two by two, through a gate. So I yelled out: "This company is dismissed for two minutes— then it will fall in again on the other side of the gate!"

But my brief experience running that company enabled me to see the cruelty of war. Chief Black Hawk had come across the Mississippi with 500 warriors in search of food. And who could blame them? They had been pushed off their homelands. Many a war has been started for lesser reasons. Marching home, I saw the remains of a skirmish at Kellogg's Grove. There I came across the first dead men I had seen. They lay together, Indian and white, their blood mingled in death. The light of the rising sun streamed upon them, painting everything red. It was grotesque. I helped to bury those men. But I could never bury that memory.

He sits at desk

I willingly gave up the life of a soldier and returned to New Salem, serving as postmaster. What I liked best about the job was that it gave me a chance to read the newspapers before I delivered them. Once, as postmaster, I received a letter, asking for the financial rating of one of my neighbors, from a big bank in New York City. I answered:

He takes the letter from the drawer of his table and reads

Sirs, I am well acquainted with him and know his circumstances. First of all, he has a wife and baby. Taken together, they should be worth $50,000 to any man. Secondly, he has an office in which there is a table worth $1.50 and three chairs worth, say, $1. Last of all, there is in one corner a large rat hole, which will bear looking into.

Yours respectfully,
A. Lincoln, Postmaster.

One day at an auction in Springfield, I bought a copy of Blackstone's *Commentaries*. And day after day, month after month, I read and reread the principles of the English common law. At first I practiced on my good neighbors—we both took our chances. But I really gained my knowledge of the law by riding the judicial circuit, from courthouse to courthouse.

Well, I went into partnership with my young friend William Herndon and together we formed the legal firm of Lincoln & Herndon. We took every case that came our way, no matter how small.

He crosses to rolltop desk; picking up pencil and file, he speaks to Herndon

Hey, Billy, this filing system could do with a little improvement. I'm going to start a new file labeled: "If Nowhere Else Look For It Here."

He sets up file on rolltop, facing audience

Strangers have often wondered how it was that I ever managed to get into politics. I did so at the same time that I practiced law. And I'll tell you this—you don't wait to be pushed forward by older men. All it takes to run for office in this country is to declare yourself. Lung power counts more than a campaign purse.

He crosses and steps up on bench, now a stump

Fellow citizens: I presume you all know who I am. I have been solicited by my friends and neighbors to stand for office in the Illinois Legislature. My opponent has alluded to the fact that I am a young man. Well, I am younger in years than I am in the tricks of politicians; but I would rather die now than, like the gentleman, live to see the day that I would have to erect a lightning rod over my house, as he has done in Springfield, to protect a guilty conscience from an offended God!

What's that, sir? No, I don't mind heckling as long as there's a question at the end of it. And in your case, sir, it doesn't even have to be an intelligent question!

My politics? Short and sweet, like the old woman's dance. I'm in favor of constructing a railroad from some point on the Illinois River to the town of Springfield. And I'm in favor of a National Bank which serves the interest of the people, instead of just making interest for the bankers. Now if elected, I promise I will bring to work a sincere heart. Whether I will bring a head equal to that heart, will be for future times to determine.

He steps off bench, and reports

Well, I lost, running eighth in a field of 13. But at least in my own village of New Salem, I received 277 out of 300 votes, and that encouraged me.

One early defeat did not turn me away from practicing politics—my lifetime preoccupation. So I ran again for the state legislature, gained office, and subsequently was elected for three further terms.

Lincoln relaxes in easy chair

To Springfield, at different times, came two Marys, both from Kentucky. Mary Owens, the daughter of a well-fixed farmer, about my age and weight. No, no, I lie, she was a little heavier. And Mary Todd, one of the Kentucky Todds. That's Todd, by the way, with two "D's." With God, one is enough, but the Todds needed two.

I courted the first one sporadically and married the second one eventually. I had made a few tentative professions of affection toward Miss Mary Owens, who was a pleasingly plump young woman. But unfortunately she left Springfield and returned to her home in Kentucky. And during the long evenings of the legislature I found myself thinking about her and wishing to see her again. And then, after three years, she returned to Springfield.

I must say I found myself stomached a little when I saw her in the flesh rather than in my imagination. I knew she was over-size, but she now appeared a fair match for Falstaff. I knew she was called an old maid, and I never doubted the first half of the description. But her age was difficult to determine, you see. Her skin was too full of fat to permit it contracting into wrinkles. And her want of teeth and weatherbeaten look gave me the notion that nothing could have commenced at the size of infancy and reached its present bulk in less than forty years. In short, I was not at all pleased with her.

I then had to write one of the most difficult letters of my life. It took a little doing to disengage myself, but I did, with her silent consent.

He leaves the chair

Between building up my law practice and serving in the legislature I had little time for the fairer sex, so it was not until the winter of 1840 that I began to pay particular court to "Molly"— Mary Todd. She was stylish, and I was, well, what you see. She came from a distinguished Kentucky family. Well, so did I. Mine was distinguished by its poverty. She had charm and personality and a long list of suitors. Once I went up to her at a dance and I said, "Miss Todd, I want to waltz with you in the worst way." And I'm afraid I did. . . .

Well, eventually, we became engaged. I wanted to impress her and her distinguished family. In fact, I even dueled for the lady. Well, at least I accepted a challenge to risk my neck gallantly, on her behalf.

Lincoln takes a few cuts with his umbrella

You see, Mary and a friend of hers, Julia Jayne, had written a series of anonymous letters to the editor of the *Sangamo Journal*. The letters were nothing more than political horseplay. But they insulted James Shields, the Illinois state auditor, accusing him of dishonesty and strutting in Springfield society. Now, Shields was a County Tyrone boy with an Irishman's short fuse— but what's worse, he was a Democrat. And the two are an explosive combination.

Well, I tried to cover up for the ladies by claiming the letters as my own. And I suppose to make matters a little worse, I offered to fight Shields with potatoes, shillelaghs or cow-dung at five paces. This only served to infuriate him. The next thing I knew, we were on a horse ferry with our seconds bound for an island across the river.

When we got there, I said to Shields, Well, I'm satisfied with these weapons if you are.

Shields hefted his cavalry broadsword. I took a few swings with mine. We glared and glowered at each other across a ten-foot plank, while our seconds tried to persuade us to call the whole thing off. "Don't you realize," they said, "dueling is against the law. The winner can be jailed. It's not going to do the loser any good either." "I know," said Shields, "but my honor must be satisfied."

He sits on the bench.

That reminds me of a story, I said. About a young Kentucky man who had enlisted in the War of 1812. He was bidding farewell to his sweetheart when she told him that she had embroidered a bullet pouch, on which she had stitched the words "Victory or Death." Well, the young soldier thought it over for awhile and he said, "Ain't that a little strong? Couldn't you write 'Victory or Be Crippled!'"

Shields didn't laugh. "Now look here, Shields," I said, "you know very well I had no intention of damaging your reputation or your standing as a gentleman."

"Are you prepared to publish a statement to that effect?"

"Yes," I said. So he stuck out his hand. We shook and returned arm-in-arm to Springfield.

Lincoln confides to audience

Now, don't circulate this story, please. I mean it's not one to put in the book of life of a political candidate. And you won't find it in mine, I promise.

When news of our dueling fiasco got back to Springfield, Mary was impressed but I was distraught. I became burdened with doubts about myself as a married man, a lawyer and a legislator—all at once. And so on New Year's day, 1841, my "Fatal First," we broke off our engagement.

He speaks to her in the empty chair. In background, we hear light, tinkling music

"Mary, it's no use trying to find out whose fault it is—yours or mine. Love isn't a court case to be won or lost. Matrimony isn't a contract, it's a conditional emotion, mutually felt."

Lincoln moves to desk, stage right

That was what I said but I felt desperate; losing her was like losing part of myself. I was miserable and sick in mind and body. I needed help and advice.

He raps on railing

Doc, are you in? It's me, Lincoln. You thought I'd be back. Thank goodness for that. Oh, Doc, I've been making a most discreditable exhibition of myself. I've had two cat fits and a duck fit. Sometimes I feel as crazy as a loon. There's a wide streak of melancholy in my soul, Doc. And now even dreams disturb my sleep. Bad dreams. Even when I turn to Shakespeare to take my mind off my melancholy, every passage seems to cry out about my own condition.

The heartaches and the thousand natural shocks that flesh is heir to . . . the pangs of despised love . . . Oh, I could be bounded in a nutshell, and count myself a king of infinite space, were it not that I have bad dreams.

I think I've even become a burden to Hamlet. I carry this little verse that I found with me. Let me read it to you, Doc.

He takes poem from waistcoat

"Oh! Why should the spirit of
  mortals be proud?
Like a swift-fleeing meteor, a
  fast-flying cloud,
A flash of the lightning,
  a break of the wave,
He passes from life to his rest
  in the grave."

He returns poem to pocket

That depresses you too, Doc. I must now be the most miserable man alive. If what I feel were equally distributed among the whole human race, there wouldn't be one cheerful face.

What's your diagnosis, then? Hypo . . . Hypochondriasis. What's that in plain language? Hellish gloom.

Well, thanks, Doc, what's this you've written underneath? Words of consolation. You put it very nobly for a friend and physician: "Melancholy is a misfortune, not a personal fault."

That's a great help; I'll remember that in the middle of the night. Thanks, Doc.

He crosses toward easy chair

About a year later, after many a night visit to Doc Henry, Simeon Francis, the editor of the *Sangamo Journal,* and his wife arranged for Molly and me to meet again.

Simeon and I had always been close, but never more so than when he opened his house for our reunion. "Be friends again," he said. When I saw Molly I realized why I had been so miserable without her.

"Mary," I said. "You look wonderful."

She returned the compliment. "Abraham," she said, "you look terrible."

We discovered there was still laughter in our hearts. We were a little older now, a little wiser, a little more tolerant of our *mutual* peculiarities.

The skies of summer brightened. And so, in the autumn of 1842, Mary Todd and Abraham Lincoln pledged their love for life. We were married. It was a source of profound wonder to me then, and it still is.

Mary Lincoln and I had four sons, all born in Springfield: Robert, Eddy, Willie and Little Tad. Each son was different, each one loveable to both of us, and all indulged by their father. Spoiled, Mary said. Mother—Mary—was the disciplinarian in our home. In fact her authority even extended over the fifth male in the household.

Lincoln puts on his waistcoat

With Mary's blessing, I decided that certain challenges existed beyond Springfield, and the Illinois General Assembly. I told some of my political friends, "If you should hear anyone say that Abe Lincoln doesn't want to go to Congress, I wish you would tell him you have reason to believe he is mistaken. The fact is I very much want to go; and do not keep this too confidential!"

He crosses and mounts the podium

Fellow citizens and members of the Seventh Congressional District: I am honored to run as your candidate and friend. My Democratic opponent, Preacher Peter Cartwright, is seizing upon false issues. He says that I openly scoff at Christianity. Now, it is true that I am not a member of any church, but I have never denied the truth of the Scriptures and I personally would not support a man for office who was an open scoffer of religion.

You know, Preacher Cartwright reminds me of another preacher from Southern Illinois, who got up in the pulpit one day and said that "our Savior was the only perfect man to have ever appeared on the earth, and there is no record in the Bible of a perfect woman."

A woman in the audience interrupted: "I know a perfect woman, and I have heard about her every day for the past 20 years." The preacher asked, "Who is she?" and she said, "My husband's first wife."

Looks toward heckler in audience

I don't think it's fair to say that. When any church will inscribe over its altar, as the sole qualification for membership, "Thou shall love the Lord with all thy heart and all thy soul and thy neighbor as thy self," that church will I join with all my heart and all my soul.

You know, I went to hear Preacher Cartwright campaign at one of his prayer meetings. He said: "All those who wish to give their hearts to God and to go to Heaven will rise." Men, women and children got to their feet. He saw me still sitting there. He said: "All those who do not wish to go to Hell will rise." Then he said: "I see that all of you save one do not wish to go to Hell. The sole exception is Mister Lincoln. May I ask, Mister Lincoln, where are you going?"

Well, Preacher Cartwright asked me directly where I'm going. Heaven or Hell? So I'm going to answer with equal directness. I would prefer not to go to either, yet. I am going to Congress!

Lincoln leaves podium

Well, what was the final count in the *Sangamo Journal?* Lincoln 6,340—Cartwright 4,829. Well, perhaps, Preacher Cartwright has now learned there's a little truth in what I said at Clinton: You can fool some of the people all the time; and you can fool all the people some of the time; but you can't fool all the people all the time.

I hope the *Sangamo Journal* and other newspapers will continue to refer to me as plain Mister Lincoln, without the Honorable in front of it. Being Honorable prevents honest or even honorable discourse between friends.

And so I prepared to take up my duties as a congressman, and I wanted to go to Washington.

The United States Supreme Court has decided, wrongly, that the Negro is a chattel, not a human being, and cannot sue for his freedom. And that the Southern States, the slave states, cannot be deprived of their human property rights. Property rights in human beings? You know, our progress in degeneracy in this country is pretty rapid. We began by declaring that all men are created equal. We now read it that all men are created equal, except Negroes.

You know, when these "Know Nothings" gain control, I think I shall prefer emigrating to some other country, where they make no pretence of loving liberty. To Russia, for example, where despotism can be taken pure, without the base alloy of hypocrisy.

It's time to draw the line. If I ever get a chance to hit the Institution of slavery, I'm going to hit it hard!

Oh, yes, I wanted to go to Washington.

Lincoln seated at table-desk

Washington, April 16, 1848.

Dear Mary,

In this troublesome world, we are never quite satisfied. When you were here, I thought you hindered me some in attending to business; but now, having nothing but business—no variety—it has grown exceedingly tasteless to me. I hate to sit down and direct documents, and I hate to stay in this old room by myself.

I went yesterday to hunt the little plaid stockings that you wanted for Eddy but I'm afraid McKnight's has quit business and Allen's had not a single pair of the description you give, and only one plaid pair of any sort that I thought would fit "Eddy's dear little feet." What did Eddy and Bobby think of the little letters father sent them? Don't let the blessed fellows forget father.

Most affectionately,
A. Lincoln.

He puts his head in his hands

Mary . . . Mary. It has returned again. My old malady, melancholia. I should be exhilarated, but depression clouds my mind. Foreboding dreams. . . .

Picking up a letter he reads

Lexington, April, 1848

My Dear Husband,

How much I wish instead of writing, we were together this evening. I feel very sad away from you. I feel weary and tired enough to know that this is Saturday night and our babies are upstairs asleep. Do not fear the children have forgotten you. I was only jesting. Even Ed's eyes brighten at the mention of your name.

Truly yours,

M. L.

In the lodging house where I lived with some of my fellow congressmen, we would sit around the fire after dinner discussing slavery. They asked me what I felt in my heart. I told them, "As I would not be a slave, so I would not be a master. This is my idea of democracy, and anything that differs from this is not democracy."

But as a freshman in the party out of power, I was able to do little toward abolishing slavery in my one term of office. And that term came to a short end after I challenged the president. President Polk's Democrats were trying to get us to justify an unjust war against Mexico. Even though I knew it would be unpopular with my constituents back home in Springfield, I felt it was my duty to speak out.

He crosses to podium

In his war message, the president declares that the soil was ours on which hostilities commenced with Mexico. But the president's evidence fails him. It is a singular fact that the president sent the army into the midst of a settlement of Mexican people. There and thereby, the first blood of the war was shed. On that very spot, the war with Mexico was unnecessarily and unconstitutionally commenced. Now, Sir, let the president answer candidly and without evasion. If he can show that the soil was ours where the first blood was shed, I shall be most happy to reverse my vote. But if he will not do this, then he is deeply conscious of being in the wrong—and he must feel that the blood of this war, like the blood of Abel, is crying to heaven against him.

Well, I guess my time is up. I gladly yield my last minute to the glorifiers of war. They will need it more than I!

He walks to rocking chair, picks up newspaper

Mary, I want to read these papers first. I'll join you and the boys in the kitchen in a few moments. Did you read the *Illinois State Register*? I expected criticism—but, Mary, this is excessive.

He reads to her

"Our district has seen many soldiers go off to war. What will these gallant men say when they learn that *their representative* has declared the cause in which they suffered was unnecessary and unconstitutional?"

He looks up

Some of them won't say anything, Mary. They'll be the silent casualties.

He continues from newspaper

"Henceforth, Lincoln will be known as the Benedict Arnold of Illinois."

He shakes his head

Branded as a traitor. Well, Mary, you're no longer the wife of a United States congressman. I can always turn to Shakespeare for solace. As the Duke of Venice says in *Othello*:

> To mourn a mischief that is past and gone
> Is the next way to draw new mischief on,
> What cannot be preserved when fortune takes,
> Patience her injury a mockery makes.

I can practice patience too, Mary, if necessary. And, if not, I can always practice law.

So it was time for me to hitch up and ride the legal circuit again and wait for new opportunities. They came sooner than I expected with the proposal to extend slavery into new territories. That burning issue aroused me to run for the United States Senate against Stephen A. Douglas.

Lincoln crosses to podium

Fellow citizens:
As this campaign continues, Judge Douglas becomes more and

more desperate. He is now trying to make capital out of the fact that I once worked in a grocery store that sold whiskey. Now, what the judge says is true. But what he didn't say was that *he* was my best customer. I've only got one small point to add: I have since left my side of the bar, while Judge Douglas still sticks to *his*.

Judge Douglas says that he is opposed to Negro citizenship. He claims that this government was made by white men, for white men and their posterity forever.

But I say there is no reason why the Negro is not entitled to every right enumerated in the Declaration of Independence, the right to life, liberty, and the pursuit of happiness.

Judge Douglas says that the Negro is not my equal. But I say in the right to eat the bread, without leave of anybody else, which his own hand earns, he is my equal and the equal of every living man!

What's that, sir? "If I love Negroes so much, why don't I marry one?" I protest against that counterfeit logic that assumes because I do not want a black woman for a slave, I must necessarily want her for a wife. I need not have her for either. I can just let her alone. No that is all I ask for the Negro. If you do not like him, let him alone. If God gave him but little, that little let him enjoy.

But I'm glad this question of intermarriage is out in the open. In 1850, there were in this country over 400,000 mulattoes. Most sprung from white masters and black slaves. In the slave State of Virginia, alone, how many do you suppose? Over 80,000. While in the state of New Hampshire, a free state, a state that goes nearer toward equality between the races than any other, there were just 185 mulattoes. So if you are worried about the mixing of the races, let me point out to you that these census figures prove that slavery itself is the greatest source of amalgamation.

These black girls are being forced into becoming the concubines of their white masters.

Friends, today closes the campaign. The planting and the culture are over, and there remains but the harvest.

If there is one single man among us who does not think that the Institution of slavery is wrong, he ought not to be with us. Slavery is a violation of the eternal right and the greatest threat to the Union. Oh yes, we have temporized with it for a hundred years because of the necessity of our condition. But as sure as God reigns, and school children read, that foul black lie can never be consecrated into God's hallowed truth.

Lincoln leaves the podium

Well, I lost—indirectly. Although the Republican State Representatives and Senators beat their Democratic opponents by some 4,000 votes, Judge Douglas won a majority in the Illinois legislature because of holdover Senators and apportionment laws. Yet from that defeat, there grew a new hope inside my mind, a new dream.

Perhaps it all began with an article that appeared in the *Chicago Tribune* which said: "Although beaten, Lincoln is now a national man and the Republican party's future spokesman."

This view seemed to be shared by the nominations committee that visited me in my home in Springfield, headed by their chairman, Jesse Fell.

Lincoln rises, offering Mr. Fell his chair

Sit down, Jesse. Are you serious, you think I could make a

formidable candidate for the presidency? I . . . I don't know what to say—and that for me is unusual. Would you like a drink? You would. Mary, would you bring in a pitcher of ice water for Jesse.

I must admit that the taste is in my mouth a little to become president, but there are other men more eligible than I. Men like Chase and Seward. Men with outspoken ideas and radical policies. My qualities are thought by many to be negative. They have long records, I have none. I was born and have ever remained in the most humble walks of life. I have no wealthy relatives to recommend me.

You mean that? That's just the sort of candidate you're looking for? Mary, you didn't put anything in that ice water, did you? Well, Jesse, if you are serious, I shall be honored to accept the nomination but I must warn you that your optimism far exceeds mine. I honestly do not feel enough of a candidate to go to the convention.

Good day to you, Jesse, and thanks for your confidence— however misplaced.

He flops into chair

Well, I did not attend the convention in Chicago. Instead I campaigned on behalf of the Republican cause. I travelled over 4,000 miles, made 23 speeches, never once expressing in public my hopes as a presidential candidate. When a not very great man is mentioned for a great position, it is apt to turn his head a little.

He picks up telegrams

The convention in Chicago lasted three days. At the end of

the first day, my backers wired me: "Very quiet, but we are moving heaven and earth." On the second day: "Keep cool, things are working." At the beginning of the third day: "Very hopeful, don't get excited." And at the end of the third day: "We did it. Glory to God. From my inmost heart I congratulate you. Jesse Fell."

In the National election the voters were pretty badly split, reflecting all the divisions in the North, in the South, and in the minds of the people.

Two ladies who were Quakers were overheard in conversation in a railway carriage: "I think Judge Douglas will be president." "Why does thee think so?" "Because Judge Douglas is a praying man." "So is Abraham Lincoln a praying man." "Yes, but the Lord will think that Mister Lincoln is joking."

Well, happily, the Lord did not think that Abraham Lincoln was joking and neither did the voters. And so I prepared to return to Washington, no longer as a one-term congressman but as president of the United States: United but divided.

Lincoln crosses to law office at rolltop desk

Hey, Billy, don't forget our new file: "If Nowhere Else, Look For It Here." You and I, we've been partners for over sixteen years. We've never had a cross word in all that time. Now I want that signboard of "Lincoln & Herndon" to remain hanging up there, undisturbed. Give our clients to understand that the election of a president makes no change in the firm of "Lincoln & Herndon." If I live, I'm coming back here one day, and you and I, Billy, we're going to keep on practicing law as if nothing happened.

He picks up carpetbag, walks downstage

My friends, No one, not in my situation, can appreciate my feeling of sadness at this parting. To this place, and the kindness of these people, I owe everything. Here I have lived a quarter of a century, and have passed from a young to an old man. Here my children have been born, and one is buried. I now leave, not knowing when, or whether ever, I may return, with a task greater than that which rested upon Washington.

I bid you an affectionate farewell.

Lincoln walks off, to his destiny

END OF ACT I

ACT II | *The Liberator*

Over the darkened stage, we hear civil war tunes. As lights come up, we see Lincoln in his shirtsleeves at home in his easy chair— now in the White House

There is one good thing about presidential elections in the United States. By the Constitution, the electors have another chance in four years.

There is one bad thing about presidential elections in the United States. The president-elect has to sit around for four months, powerless to control events.

When I arrived in Washington, the sound of intermittent gunfire already filled the air. At that moment of excitement and expectancy, I did not know that another destiny awaited Abraham Lincoln, less than five years later. Even then we were not all agreed as to what the administration should do, or how it should be done. Some people seemed to think the moment I became president I had the power to abolish slavery, forgetting that I first had to take the oath to uphold the Constitution of the United

States. The paramount idea of the Constitution is the preservation of the Union. For without the Union, the Constitution would be useless.

Over one-seventh of the population were slaves, not distributed generally over the Union, but localized in the southern part of it. Now these slaves constituted a powerful commercial interest. To strengthen, perpetuate and extend this interest was the reason for which the insurgents were prepared to rend the Union even by war.

Lincoln leaves chair, puts on waistcoat

They called themselves the Confederates, but I called them disunionists. They reminded me of the gambler who was playing cards for high stakes. He suspected his adversary of foul play, and suddenly drew his bowie knife from his belt and pinned the hand of the other player upon the table, exclaiming: "If you haven't got the ace of spades under your palm, I'll apologise."

He looks at the mirror in the hallstand

Ah, Mr. Nicolay. Tell me, do you think people will say that these chin-whiskers of mine are just a silly piece of affectation? You don't have to answer that too truthfully—I cannot expect official loyalty from my secretary to include my new beard. The boys quite like it, but Mary hasn't cast her chin-whiskers vote yet.

You know, this reminds me of the time I was working as a flatboatman in New Salem. And there was a big Chicago lawyer passing through the village. Well, one morning I rested my elbows on the bureau in front of the looking glass and I stared at myself. It struck me what an ugly man I was. It made me so mad, I vowed that if I ever met an uglier man, I would shoot him on sight.

Well, this big Chicago lawyer stopped off at the Rutledge Tavern. I said to myself, "There's your man." Pointing my gun at him, I told him to say his prayers. "Why, Lincoln?" he said, "What have I done?" I told him of my vow. "Lincoln," he said, "do you really think I'm uglier than you?" "Yes," I said. "In that case, Lincoln," he replied, "If I'm uglier than you, fire away!"

Ah, Mr. Nicolay, don't look so shocked. You don't have to swallow my stories wholesale. I've told you before, I'm only a *retail* dealer.

He picks up hat and umbrella

Well, Nicolay, wish me luck with my inaugural speech. The hour is very late but I hope my words can stop the clock of war.

I've always hated the idea of war. It fixes the public gaze on parading and preening and makes heroes out of generals. I do not appreciate this matter of rank. And I surely do not believe that the military profession should mix in politics. War glorifies militarism—that attractive rainbow, rising in showers of blood.

Lincoln on presidential podium

Fellow citizens of the United States:

This country, with its institutions, belongs to the people who inhabit it. Whenever they shall grow weary of the existing government, they can exercise their *constitutional* right of amending it, or their *revolutionary* right to dismember and overthrow it.

My countrymen, one and all, take time and think well. Nothing valuable can be lost by taking time.

Plainly, the central idea of secession is the very essence of anarchy.

Physically speaking, we cannot separate. We cannot remove our respective sections from each other, nor build an impassable wall between them. A husband and wife may be divorced, and go out of the presence, and beyond the reach of each other; but the different parts of our country cannot do this. They cannot but remain face to face; and intercourse, either amicable or hostile, must continue between them.

In your hands, my dissatisfied fellow countrymen, and not in mine, is the momentous issue of civil war. The government will not assail you, unless you first assail it. You can have no conflict, without being yourselves the aggressors. You have no oath registered in Heaven to destroy this government, while I have the most solemn one to "preserve, protect and defend" it. With you, and not with me, is the solemn question: Shall it be peace or a sword?

We are not enemies but friends. We must not be enemies. Though passion may have strained, it must not break our bonds of affection. The mystic chords of memory, stretching from every battlefield and patriot grave, to every living heart and hearthstone, all over this broad land, will yet swell the chorus of the Union, when again touched, as surely they will be, by the better angels of our nature.

He steps down and tells audience:

Well, my speech went down reasonably well, but it could not halt the juggernaut of war. Over a quarter of a million men were assembled in the Army of the Potomac, commanded by General George McClellan, who thought he was a little Napoleon, because the papers told him so. Not far away, the Army of North Virginia was forming, over a hundred thousand strong, led by General Robert E. Lee. The armies faced each other, the Blue versus the Gray.

Washington became an armed camp. War knows no holidays but that is how the Civil War began. Some civilians actually carried picnic lunches from Washington to watch the first battle across the Potomac at a little creek called Bull Run. Our retreat was led by a scared, fast-running congressman with his coattails flying.

Lincoln at telegraph office desk, stage right. Telegraph is clicking

The military telegraph office was where I heard the news of the first battle—mostly bad.

Good morning, boys, still deciphering the dispatches from General McClellan? What's his latest? "We have captured six cows. What shall we do with them?" Send him this reply, Captain Eckert. As to the six captured cows—please milk them.

Regarding your dispatch about sore-tongued and fatigued horses. Will you pardon me for asking what the horses in your army have done that should fatigue anything? A. Lincoln.

The trouble with McClellan is he has the slows. Why I'd even hold his horse for him if he'd win some battles for me. But I'm afraid McClellan doesn't know the difference between a chestnut horse and a horse chestnut.

He picks up another dispatch

More news from the front.

Now General Pope says he has retired to Centerville where he will be able to *hold* his men. I don't like that attitude. I don't like to hear that his men need holding.

Send him this reply: General Pope. If you do not want to use your army in battle, may I borrow it for a while? A. Lincoln.

He turns in a confidential aside outside the telegraph office

Ah! Secretary Seward. Tell me, how go your State Department negotiations for the services of General Garibaldi? He's the greatest guerrilla fighter in Europe today, and that is the kind of war Johnny Reb is fighting in Virginia. Tell him that he will receive a major general's commission in our army, and a hearty welcome from the American people.

But for reasons of diplomacy, leave my name out of dealings. We don't want to upset our delicate balance with the European governments. Yes, I know it's a long shot, Mr. Secretary, but it's worth trying—in *your* name.

He returns to the telegraph office

All right, boys, just one or two more and I won't bother you for a few hours.

To Major General John Pope:

I have heard of your recently saying that both the army and the government needed a dictator. It was, of course, not for this remark but in spite of it that I am allowing you to keep your command. Only generals who gain successes can set up dictators. What I now ask of you is military success and *I* will risk the dictatorship. And please, General Pope, do not send me anymore of these urgent dispatches datelined: "Headquarters in the saddle."

He pauses, then comments for the audience

Your trouble is, you have your *headquarters* where your *hind-quarters* ought to be.

Lincoln moves to his desk downstage

Mr. Nicolay, will you take a letter please.

To the Honorable Horace Greeley, *New York Tribune.* As to the policy you say I seem to be pursuing, I do not mean to leave you or anyone else in any doubt. I would save the Union the shortest way under the Constitution. If I could save it by not freeing any slaves, I would do it, and if I could save the union by freeing all the slaves I would do it, and if I could save it by freeing some and leaving others alone, I would also do that. I have stated my purpose according to my view of *official* duty; but I intend no modification of my oft-expressed *personal* view that all men, everywhere, should be free.

Would you send that off ahead of everything else, please. And make a copy for the Washington newspapers so he can read it there, first.

Lincoln strides across stage to his White House chair, at home with Mary. He raises his voice

Mary, after all these years you are still a child-wife needing protection from flattering storekeepers! You seem to have out-fitted yourself with an entire issue of *Godey's Lady's Book.*

Satin bonnets, black laces from Europe, gloves by the dozen. You know, you are the best friend of the New York merchants! And now this for wallpaper. You have overrun an appropriation by $6,500 for decorating the White House. I cannot possibly approve of this—I'll pay for it out of my own pocket first! It would stink in the nostrils of the American people to have it said that the president had approved an appropriation for flubdubs, for this damned old house, while the soldiers have no blankets!

Now, Mary, let's have no more of these extravagances.

He calms down

Mary, I now have to deal with the most urgent business that will ever cross my desk in the White House: Emancipating the Negroes.

When I go into my cabinet meeting, I shall present them with the proclamation of freedom. I have an argument which even those who still waver will find difficult to oppose. It is simply this: By putting the black man in Union blue, we will so increase our fighting power that the death knell will be sounded for the Confederacy and for slavery itself. It will help win the war sooner and save lives. With all my heart, I believe that those perpetuating slavery are blowing out the moral lights around us.

Do you remember, Mary, when we talked of abolishing slavery back in Springfield, I said that if I ever got a chance to hit the Institution, I would hit it hard. But the time was not yet ripe. Now it is, because of military *and* moral necessity. The moment has come.

Lincoln crosses and sits at his desk

Be seated, gentlemen. First, let us deal with a nettlesome matter that has become one of my most unpopular acts in your state courts. I refer to the suspending of habeas corpus, so that these traitors who have been arrested as subversives to our Union cause cannot be freed simply by a court order. Now if you think I should continue to suspend habeas corpus without congressional approval, please say "aye."

He repeats each reply, turning to every cabinet member

Secretary of State Seward? Nay.
Treasury Secretary Chase? Nay.
Secretary of War Stanton? Nay.
Attorney General Bates? Nay.
What say you, Postmaster General Blair? Nay.
And you, Navy Secretary Welles? Nay.
Finally, Interior Secretary Smith? Nay.

Lincoln points to each man and repeats their nays. Then:

Well, gentlemen, the *Ayes* have it.

I am sorry, gentlemen, but these subversives are mad dogs who would stop at nothing if they were released.

That reminds me of a story. About a man who was walking along a country lane with a pitchfork over his shoulder. Just as he was passing this farm house, a mad dog rushed out and attacked him. So the man killed the dog with the pitchfork. The angry farmer asked, "Why did you kill my dog?" "Well, why did your dog attack me?" "Why didn't you fend him off with the blunt end?" "Why didn't your dog attack me with his blunt end?"

What's that, Mr. Welles? How can I indulge in such levity at this time? Sir, if I did not take some momentary respite from the crushing burden I am carrying, I think my heart would break.

And now, Gentlemen, we come to a much greater matter—the need for a proclamation to emancipate the Negroes.

He pulls a clipping from his pocket

If you have not seen this little poem by James Russell Lowell that I clipped out of the *Boston Atlas*, let me read it to you:

> "Ef you take a sword and dror it
> An stick a fellow creatur thru
> Gov'ment hain't to answer for it
> God'll send the bill to you."

God'll send the bill. Well, gentlemen, the Confederates are getting their bill now for a hundred years of the lash. I have distributed copies of this Emancipation Proclamation to each one of you before I sign it now.

He picks up pen, hesitates, puts it down

I never in my life felt more certain that I was doing right than I do in signing this paper. But I have been receiving calls and shaking hands, since nine o'clock this morning, till my arm is stiff and numb. Now this signature is one that will be closely examined, and if people believe my hand trembled they will say, "He had compunctions." But, anyway, it is going to be done.

He raises pen and signs deliberately

Gentlemen, it is done!

We are now like whalers who have been on a long chase. At last we've got our harpoon into the monster, but we have to steer very carefully because with one flip of his tail, he could send us all into eternity.

Lincoln puts on spectacles, steps on podium with document and reads

A Proclamation:

I so order and declare that all persons held as slaves henceforward shall be forever free, and that the government will recognise and maintain the freedom of said persons. I hereby enjoin upon the people so declared to be free to abstain from all violence, unless in necessary self-defense. And I recommend to them that, in all cases when allowed, they labor fruitfully for reasonable wages. I further declare that all such persons will be received into the armed services of the United States. And upon this act, sincerely believed to be an act of justice, warranted by the Constitution, upon military necessity, I invoke the considerate judgement of mankind, and the gracious favor of Almighty God.

He leaves the podium and picks up paper from newspaper rack near his easy chair

A wave of fury swept the South. The *Richmond Enquirer* said, "Lincoln is outraging private property rights. He is inciting Negroes to rape burn and kill. He is breaking all the laws of civilized warfare. . . ."

Civilized warfare? *There's* a contradiction. Between May

2nd and 4th at Chancellorsville, the Union lost over 17,000 men while the Confederates lost over 12,000. In less than three days nearly 30,000 boys, brothers in blue and gray, cut down by bullets and bayonets.

He sits on front bench, his head in his hands. Then he looks up, reciting softly to himself

> O, my offence is rank, it smells to heaven;
> It hath the primal eldest curse upon't,
> A brother's murder. Pray can I not,
> Though inclination be as sharp as will:
> My stronger guilt defeats my strong intent . . .
> What if this cursed hand were thicker than
>   itself with brother's blood,
> Is there not rain enough in the sweet heavens,
> To wash it white as snow?"

He looks up, tearfully

But why should God forgive me rather than the Confederate leaders? Both parties prayed to the same God and each invoked God's aid against the other. In this Civil War, I think God's purpose may be entirely different from that of either party. No family is immune from tragedy along the battle routes of the South. Including my own. Mary has lost three brothers, killed in the War. Now that our little Willie has died in the White House the frightened look in Mary's eyes when I enter a room appalls me. If anything should happen to Robert, Tad, or me, I think it would drive her mad. Still, I am forced to defend her against slanderous attack.

He crosses behind railing on right. Angrily:

I, Abraham Lincoln, president of these United States, appear of my own volition before this Joint Committee on the Conduct of the War, to say the following: I, to my own knowledge, know it is grossly untrue that my wife holds treasonable communication with the enemy. This is a vicious rumour! She is as loyal as I! I totally disavow this outrageous charge.

He moves to center of stage

But persecution was in the air. After further Union disasters at Fredericksburg, my own Republican senators met in secret caucus to vote on a resolution asking me to resign. But I knew the country's fortunes and my own were bound together, that if I were to relinquish my post it would spell certain and inevitable ruin for our country. And so I carried on with my everyday routine at the White House.

Each day at noon, I ordered the doors to be opened, and the people waiting outside were admitted. They would line up to plead for clemency for their husbands and sons in uniform, to seek jobs, or just to pour their hearts out. It gave me a chance to meet the people.

One gentleman pleaded with me for a pass to go through our lines to the enemy capital, Richmond. I told him: "My dear Sir, I would be most happy to oblige you if my passes were respected, but the fact is that, within the last two years, I have given passes to more than 250,000 men in the Army of the Potomac to go to Richmond and not one has got there yet!"

Many an old lawyer from the 8th Judicial Circuit came to visit me when I was in Washington. I remember one old friend asked me: "How does it feel to be president?" I said, That reminds me of a story—about the man who was tarred and feathered and ridden out of town on a rail. Someone asked him how he liked it. He replied, "Well, if it wasn't for the honor of the thing, I would much rather have walked!"

The war of attrition had become total war. No family was immune from tragedy along the battle routes of the South. Houses were burned, railroads ripped up, mills and factories destroyed, cotton put to the torch, cattle and provisions foraged. Oh, yes, our soldiers had become well-versed in the art of destruction.

But at last I had found my general in Grant. He realized that our main objective was not Southern real estate but General Lee's Army. He had his critics after Shiloh because of the heavy casualties. But I couldn't spare that man—he fought. People said he drank too much; but if drink could make him fight as he did it was time to send a few barrels of his particular brand of whiskey to the other generals.

I only had one small difficulty with General Grant. He issued Order No. 11, expelling all Jews from the Union camps. I had no objection to expelling traitors and Jewish peddlers who defied military regulations. But Order No. 11 proscribed an entire religious class, and many members of the Hebrew faith were fighting with great gallantry in our ranks. This was indefensible. I revoked General Grant's order, with no objection from him when I told him why, and that ended the temporary injustice.

He picks up papers on his desk

Here's another batch of requests for pardons from men awaiting to be shot for desertion. My generals say that I impair Army discipline, but it relieves me if I can find an excuse to save another man's life.

Ah, Mr. Nicolay. Please inscribe these messages and get them off without delay:

To the secretary of war. My Dear Sir: Regarding the 14-year-old soldier sentenced to be shot for desertion, instead let us spank this drummer boy, and send him home.

Yes, Mr. Nicolay, just as I dictated it.

Here's another to the secretary of war. Please suspend execution in this group of "leg cases." The army expression is "cowardice in the face of the enemy," but I prefer to call them for short, my "leg cases." I put it to you: If God gave a man a pair of cowardly legs, how can he help them running away with him?

Telegraph this to Major General Sheridan in the field: Suspend execution in this case and send record of trial to me for further examination. If a man had more than one life, I believe a little hanging would not hurt this one, but as he has only one life, I think I will pardon him. A. Lincoln.

He crosses up to the telegraph table

The grim news from Gettysburg started to arrive in Washington. Gettysburg should have been the last battle! We had Lee's army bottled up, but they got away. We buried 6,832 men at Gettysburg. I was asked to make a few appropriate remarks to dedicate the military cemetery.

He crosses down center and stands on stump as the lights fade. Taps are first heard softly in the background. Then:

Four score and seven years ago, our fathers brought forth on this continent, a new nation, conceived in liberty, and dedicated to the proposition that all men are created equal.

Now we are engaged in a great civil war, testing whether that nation, or any nation so conceived and so dedicated, can long endure. We are met on a great battlefield of that war. We have come to dedicate a portion of that field, as a final resting place for those who here gave their lives that that nation might live. It is altogether fitting and proper that we should do this.

But in a larger sense, we cannot dedicate—we cannot consecrate—we cannot hallow—this ground. The brave men, living and dead, who struggled here, have consecrated it, far above our poor power to add or detract. The world will little note, nor long remember what we say here, but it can never forget what they did here. It is for us the living, rather, to be dedicated here to the great task remaining before us—that from these honored dead we take increased devotion to that cause for which they gave the last full measure of devotion—that we here highly resolve that these dead shall not have died in vain—that this nation, under God, shall have a new birth of freedom—and that government of the people, by the people, for the people, shall not perish from the earth.

A gun salute fires. He steps off the stump and crosses to the telegraph office

The battles and the bloodletting continued for almost a year and a half after the dedication at Gettysburg. But the outcome was inevitable; the North had the manpower, the industry and the cause of freedom on its side: while the Rebellion had only a dying dream of a separate government for Dixie Land.

He picks up a telegram from the table

On Palm Sunday, April 9th, at 4:30 p.m., Grant telegraphed Stanton: "General Robert E. Lee surrendered the Army of Northern Virginia this afternoon on terms proposed by myself."

He steps downstage and leans on the railing while music plays softly in the background

The war was over.

He walks upstage around the railing to the bench

After four years of civil strife, the death roll on both sides amounted to over half a million men. General Grant allowed the surrendered men in Gray to take their mules and their horses and return home for spring plowing.

It was a time to plant seeds, not men, in the American soil.

He kneels at bench

But I could not forget the Kentucky father who lost both his sons, one dying for the North, one dying for the South. Over their joint graves the father had inscribed: "God knows which was right."

He rises

The hatred festered by the violent years would not quickly heal. The sacrifices would not easily be forgotten—but, at least, the slaughter had ceased—and the bitterness would eventually dissolve into the realms of memory.

Sounds of crowds are heard

A new dawn rose over Washington, with the boom of cannon. Through the gaslit, muddy streets the crowds surged toward the White House. Civilians linked arms with mud-splattered veterans who had marched from the Mississippi through the shellholes of Shiloh. Brass bands blared and, over the strident jubilation, I could hear the cries for Father Abraham.

But Father Abraham could only think of grieving families, all over our land, of the tens of thousands of dead soldier boys who could not share this moment of celebration after long winters of war.

On the balcony of the White House, Tad held a captured Confederate flag. Cheers rocketed skywards as he waved the Stars and Bars. Below me, in the shadows, I could see Negro soldiers standing on guard, rifles at the ready, dressed in Union blue. The language of the Emancipation had become a reality. As the heaving mass of laughing, crying humanity quieted down, I said: "I propose closing this interview by asking the band to play a particular tune. I have always thought 'Dixie' one of the best tunes I have ever heard."

Dixie begins playing. After the first few bars it begins to fade as the lights come down to Lincoln's head

With malice toward none; with charity for all; with firmness in the right, as God gives us to see the right, let us strive on to